Awesome Ancient Animals

Saber Tooths Are the Big Cats

Ice Age

Dougal Dixon

An Hachette Company

First published in the United States by
New Forest Press, an imprint of Octopus Publishing Group Ltd

www.octopusbook.usa.com

Published by arrangement with Black Rabbit Books

PO Box 784, Mankato, MN 56002

Library of Congress Cataloging-in-Publication Data

Dixon, Dougal.
Saber Tooths are the Big Cats : Ice Age / by Dougal Dixon.
p. cm. -- (Awesome Ancient Animals)
Summary: "Describes the animals of the Quaternary Period, when
an Ice Age took hold of Earth, and new animals evolved to survive
the harsh weather. This period also marks when our human
ancestors started to appear. Includes an Animal Families glossary,
prehistory timeline, and pronunciation guides"-- Provided by
publisher.
Includes index.
ISBN 978-1-84898-627-5 (hardcover, library bound)
1. Paleontology--Pleistocene--Juvenile literature. 2. Animals,
Fossil--Juvenile literature. I. Title.
QE741.2.D594 2013
560'.1792--dc23
2012002748

Printed and bound in the USA

16 15 14 13 12 1 2 3 4 5

Publisher: Tim Cook Editor: Margaret Parrish Designer: Steve West

Contents

Introduction

This is how the Earth looked in the Quaternary Period. The white areas show how much of the Earth was covered in glaciers.

This map shows how the Earth looks today. See how different it is! The continents have split up and moved around.

Awesome Ancient Animals follows the evolution of animals.

Earth's history is divided into sections called eras, which are divided into periods. These last millions of years. *Saber Tooths Are the Big Cats* takes you back to the Quarternary Period, when an Ice Age took hold of the Earth and changed its climate. New animals evolved that could survive the harsh weather. During this period, our first human ancestors appeared.

A LOOK BACK IN TIME

This timeline shows how simple creatures evolved into many differnt and complex life-forms. This took millions and millions of years. In the chart, MYA stands for million years ago.

	BOOK	PERIOD	
CENOZOIC ERA	**THE ICE AGE**	1.81 MYA to now QUATERNARY	This is a time of Ice Ages and mammals. Our direct relatives, Homo sapiens, appear.
	ANCIENT MAMMALS	65 to 1.81 MYA TERTIARY	Giant mammals and huge, hunting birds rule. Our first human relatives start to evolve.
MESOZOIC ERA	**CRETACEOUS LIFE**	145 to 65 MYA CRETACEOUS	Huge dinosaurs evolve. They die out by the end of this period.
	JURASSIC LIFE	200 to 145 MYA JURASSIC	Large and small dinosaurs and flying creatures develop.
	TRIASSIC LIFE	250 to 200 MYA TRIASSIC	The "Age of Dinosaurs begins. Early mammals live alongside them.
PALEOZOIC ERA	**EARLY LIFE**	299 to 250 MYA PERMIAN	Sail-backed reptiles start to appear.
		359 to 299 MYA CARBONIFEROUS	The first reptiles appear and tropical forests develop.
		416 to 359 MYA DEVONIAN	Bony fish evolve. Trees and insects come on the scene.
		444 to 416 MYA SILURIAN	Fish with jaws develop and sea animals start living on land.
		488 to 444 MYA ORDOVICIAN	Primitive fish, trilobites, shellfish, and plants evolve.
		542 to 488 MYA CAMBRIAN	First animals with skeletons appear.

Megalania

When the first people arrived in Australia 40,000 years ago they must have been terrified of *Megalania*. This gigantic lizard was a fierce predator. It had sharp teeth and big claws and hunted by ambush. It waited until its prey was close, then attacked.

Megalania probably hunted in short bursts of speed. Like other reptiles, Megalania could not control its body temperature. If it ran too fast it overheated.

Scientists have not found a full skeleton of *Megalania*. The bones that have been discovered suggest that it had a short, massive body.

Animal fact file

NAME: MEGALANIA (GREAT RIPPER)

PRONOUNCED: MEG-AL-AI-NEE-AH

GROUP: VARANID LIZARDS

WHERE IT LIVED: AUSTRALIA

WHEN IT LIVED: EARLY QUATERNARY PERIOD (1.6 MILLION TO 40,000 YEARS AGO)

LENGTH: 18 FT (5.5 M)

SPECIAL FEATURES: THE BIGGEST LIZARD THAT HAS EVER EXISTED

FOOD: MEAT FROM ANIMALS IT CAUGHT ITSELF OR SCAVENGED FROM DEAD BODIES

MAIN ENEMY: CARNIVOROUS MARSUPIALS, SUCH AS THYLACOLEO

DID YOU KNOW?: MEGALANIA WOULD HAVE TACKLED PREY UP TO TEN TIMES ITS SIZE. IT COULD HAVE HUNTED THE BIGGEST ANIMALS IN AUSTRALIA AT THE TIME.

Dinornis

Before people reached New Zealand—about 1,000 years ago—bats were the only mammals living there. A vast range of ground-dwelling birds, known as the moas, did inhabit the islands. The biggest was *Dinornis*. It is the heaviest bird to have lived.

In the Quaternary Period, New Zealand was covered in forest. *Dinornis* had a short, broad beak. It was ideal for rooting through forest undergrowth to find the tastiest food.

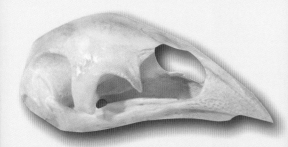

The moa usually held its head close to the ground so it could search for food. It looked up to scan for danger.

Animal fact file

NAME: DINORNIS
(TERRIBLE BIRD)

PRONOUNCED: DIE-NOR-NIS

GROUP: RATITES—FLIGHTLESS BIRDS

WHERE IT LIVED:
NEW ZEALAND

WHEN IT LIVED: THROUGHOUT THE QUATERNARY PERIOD (1.6 MILLION TO 200 YEARS AGO)

HEIGHT: 6 FT 6 IN (2 M) AT THE MIDPOINT OF THE BACK

SPECIAL FEATURES: GIANT FLIGHTLESS BIRD WITH A TINY HEAD AND ENORMOUS LEGS

FOOD: TWIGS, BERRIES, AND LEAVES. IT SWALLOWED STONES TO GRIND UP THE FOOD

MAIN ENEMY: PEOPLE, AND A KIND OF GIANT EAGLE THAT LIVED IN NEW ZEALAND

DID YOU KNOW?: THERE WERE 11 SPECIES OF MOA, SOME THE SIZE OF A TURKEY. HUMANS HUNTED MOAS TO EXTINCTION A FEW HUNDRED YEARS AGO.

Thylacoleo

Most of the mammals of Australia are marsupials—they carry their young in pouches. The different types of modern marsupial are tree climbers (koalas), grass-eaters (kangaroos), and burrow-dwellers (wombats). In the Quaternary Period there was a marsupial version of the lion—*Thylacoleo*.

The strong front legs and big thumb claw of *Thylacoleo* suggest that it ambushed its prey. It waited in overhanging branches until it could leap down, wrestling its victim to the ground and killing it by slashing and biting.

The muscle attachments on the jaws of *Thylacoleo* show that it had the strongest bite of any known mammal. Its bite was about the same as an African lion's—although it was half the size.

Animal fact file

NAME: THYLACOLEO (POUCHED LION)

PRONOUNCED: THY-LAC-OH-LEE-OH

GROUP: MARSUPIAL MAMMALS

WHERE IT LIVED: AUSTRALIA

WHEN IT LIVED: LATE TERTIARY PERIOD TO THE EARLY QUATERNARY PERIOD (24 MILLION TO 30,000 YEARS AGO)

LENGTH: 4 FT (1.2 M)

SPECIAL FEATURES: KILLING TEETH AT THE FRONT AND HUGE MEAT-SHEARING TEETH AT THE BACK

FOOD: BIG MARSUPIAL MAMMALS

MAIN ENEMY: NONE

DID YOU KNOW?: SCIENTISTS FIRST THOUGHT THAT THYLACOLEO WAS A PLANT-EATER AND ITS BIG TEETH WERE FOR SPLITTING HARD FRUIT. MOST NOW AGREE IT WAS A MEAT-EATER.

Megatherium

A sloth today is a small animal—about the size of a medium-sized dog. It hangs upside down from trees and eats leaves. In prehistoric times, some sloths were as big as elephants. They were much too large to live in trees. They had huge claws that could rip away at branches and pull down high trees to feed. *Megatherium* was the biggest of these ground sloths.

This *Megatherium* had broad hip bones and massive hind legs. It probably sat, as solid and stable as a pyramid, while reaching up to snatch leaves and twigs from trees.

The first people in South America hunted these great beasts for food. One animal could feed a whole tribe.

Animal fact file

NAME: MEGATHERIUM (GREAT BEAST)

PRONOUNCED: MEG-AH-THEER-EE-UM

GROUP: XENARTHRAN MAMMALS

WHERE IT LIVED: SOUTH AMERICA

WHEN IT LIVED: EARLY TO MID QUATERNARY PERIOD (1.9 MILLION TO 8,000 YEARS AGO)

LENGTH: 20 FT (6 M)

SPECIAL FEATURES: HUGE CLAWS ON FRONT AND HIND FEET; SHAGGY FUR

FOOD: SHOOTS AND LEAVES, ALTHOUGH SOME SCIENTISTS THINK THEY HAD BIG CLAWS BECAUSE THEY WERE MEAT-EATERS

MAIN ENEMY: CARNIVOROUS MAMMALS SUCH AS SMILODON

DID YOU KNOW?: IN THE 19TH CENTURY IT WAS THOUGHT THAT EARLY PEOPLES FARMED MEGATHERIUM BY WALLING THEM UP IN CAVES. IN FACT, THE ANIMALS WERE TRAPPED NATURALLY BY ROCK FALLS.

Doedicurus

Doedicurus looked like an armadillo but was the size of a car. The glyptodonts evolved in South America in Early Quaternary times, while the continent was still an island. *Doedicurus* was shaped like most of the other glyptodonts, but it had a fearsome, spiked club on the end of its tail.

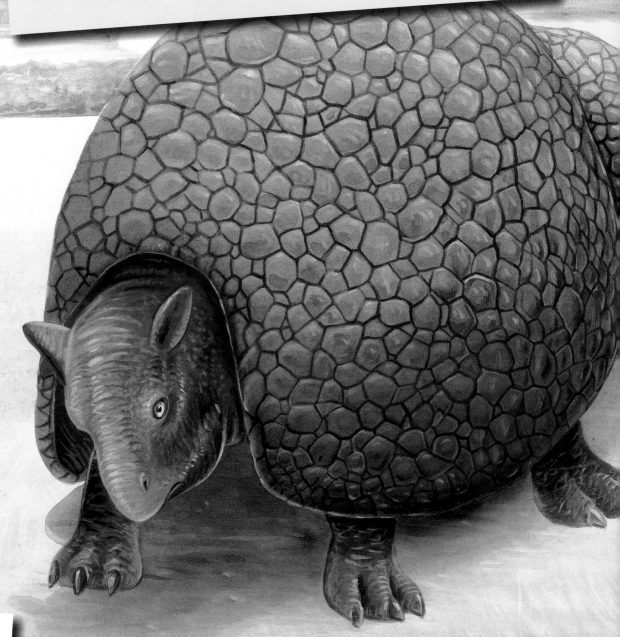

Doedicurus had solid armor made of small pieces of bone joined together. Around the joints, gaps between the pieces made the armor flexible—like the chain mail worn by medieval knights.

Doedicurus had a stiff, straight tail. It only bent at the base, which made it very strong. Doedicurus would have swung the tail with great force from its powerful hips.

Animal fact file

NAME: DOEDICURUS (PESTLE TAIL)

PRONOUNCED: DOE-DIC-ER-US

GROUP: GLYPTODONT— XENARTHRAN MAMMALS

WHERE IT LIVED: SOUTH AMERICA

WHEN IT LIVED: EARLY QUATERNARY PERIOD (2 MILLION TO 15,000 YEARS AGO)

LENGTH: 13 FT (4 M)

SPECIAL FEATURES: SHELL ON THE BACK AND SPIKED TAIL CLUB

FOOD: PLANTS

MAIN ENEMY: NONE

DID YOU KNOW?: SCIENTISTS USED TO THINK THAT GLYPTODONTS LIKE DOEDICURUS ONLY RECENTLY BECAME EXTINCT. THIS IS BECAUSE ITS THICK, STRONG ARMOR WAS SO WELL PRESERVED THAT IT DIDN'T LOOK LIKE IT WAS TENS OF THOUSANDS OF YEARS OLD!

Megaloceros

Modern moose and elk have spectacular antlers. However, these are tiny compared with the antlers of the big Ice Age deer *Megaloceros*. Each antler would have been about 5 feet (1.5 meters). Only males had antlers. They used them to attract females and fight off rivals.

Megaloceros lived throughout Europe, but it was particularly common in Ireland, where it had no predators and plenty of food. The antlers of *Megaloceros* are frequently found in Irish peat bogs, which is why it is also called the Great Irish Elk.

The leader of the *Megaloceros* herd must have been a magnificent sight, watching over his herd and protecting it against other males. However, it could not guard against early human hunters. By the end of the Ice Age *Megaloceros* was extinct.

Animal fact file

NAME: MEGALOCEROS (GIANT HORN)

PRONOUNCED: MEG-AH-LOSS-ER-OSS

GROUP: ARTIODACTYLS

WHERE IT LIVED: EUROPE AND WESTERN ASIA

WHEN IT LIVED: MID QUATERNARY PERIOD (1.5 MILLION TO 11,000 YEARS AGO)

HEIGHT: 10 FT (3 M)

SPAN OF ANTLERS: 11 FT (3.3 M). TODAY, THE LARGEST MOOSE ANTLERS SPAN ABOUT 6 FT 6 IN (2 M).

SPECIAL FEATURES: HUGE ANTLERS WERE SHED AND REGROWN EACH YEAR

FOOD: GRASS AND VEGETATION

MAIN ENEMY: EARLY HUMANS

DID YOU KNOW?: MEGALOCEROS NEEDED CERTAIN MINERALS TO REGROW ITS ANTLERS EACH YEAR. WHEN THE CLIMATE GOT COLDER THE PLANTS THAT PROVIDED THESE MINERALS BECAME SCARCE. HUMANS ALSO OVERHUNTED MEGALOCEROS.

Mammuthus

Probably the most famous of the Ice Age mammals is the woolly mammoth, with its long shaggy hair and massive curved tusks. Unlike today's elephants, which live in hot climates, the mammoth was adapted to the cold.

The thick hair of the mammoth protected it from the cold. The hump on its shoulders contained a food supply of fat that would see it through the harsh winters. The massive tusks were used to scrape snow off the mosses, lichens and grasses it ate.

Sometimes mammoths became buried in mud when they sank into a peat bog. This mud later froze. Completely frozen bodies of mammoths thousands of years old have been found.

Animal fact file

NAME: MAMMUTHUS (BURROWING ONE)

PRONOUNCED: MAM-UTH-US

GROUP: ELEPHANTS

WHERE IT LIVED: CANADA, ALASKA, SIBERIA, AND NORTHERN EUROPE

WHEN IT LIVED: LATE TERTIARY PERIOD TO LATE QUATERNARY PERIOD (4.8 MILLION YEARS AGO TO 2,500 YEARS AGO)

HEIGHT: 9 FT (2.7 M) AT THE SHOULDERS

SPECIAL FEATURES: ADAPTATIONS FOR A COLD CLIMATE

FOOD: GRASSES, LICHENS, AND MOSSES

MAIN ENEMY: HUMANS

DID YOU KNOW?: MAMMOTHS WERE NAMED "BURROWING ONE" BECAUSE WHEN THEIR BONES WERE FIRST FOUND IN SIBERIA, THE LOCAL PEOPLE THOUGHT THAT THEY WERE THE REMAINS OF ANIMALS THAT LIVED UNDERGROUND.

Coelodonta

The woolly rhinoceros, *Coelodonta*, is a familiar Ice Age mammal. It roamed the freezing northern plains of Europe and Asia, either on its own or in small family groups. Like the woolly mammoth, it was adapted to cold conditions, even though its modern-day relatives live in tropical areas.

Shaggy hair protected *Coelodonta* from the cold. It had short legs and small ears, so these parts of its body were kept warm.

A bony structure in its nose supported the weight of *Coelodonta's* horn, which was made of compacted hair. Males and females had horns. They used them like snowplows to move snow and get at the grass underneath.

Animal fact file

NAME: COELODONTA (HOLLOW TOOTH)

PRONOUNCED: SEE-LOW-DONT-AH

GROUP: PERISSODACTYLS

WHERE IT LIVED: NORTHERN EUROPE AND ASIA

WHEN IT LIVED: EARLY TO MID QUATERNARY PERIOD (1.8 MILLION TO 20,000 YEARS AGO)

LENGTH: 11 FT (3.3 M)

SPECIAL FEATURES: TWO HORNS, ONE OF WHICH WAS 3 FT (1 M) LONG

FOOD: GRASS

MAIN ENEMY: HUMANS

DID YOU KNOW?: EARLY PEOPLE HUNTED THE WOOLY RHINOCEROS AND DREW PICTURES OF IT ON CAVE WALLS IN CENTRAL EUROPE.

Smilodon

Saber-tooth cats hunted big animals during the Quaternary Period. A saber is a curved sword, and that is just what *Smilodon's* long front teeth were like. They could easily slash through thick skin and muscle. *Smilodon* was the biggest of the saber-tooth cats.

Smilodon was not fast. It ambushed its prey and wounded it fatally. The injured animal would bleed to death.

Smilodon's huge canine teeth were killing weapons. They killed by slashing their prey, not biting it as modern cats do.

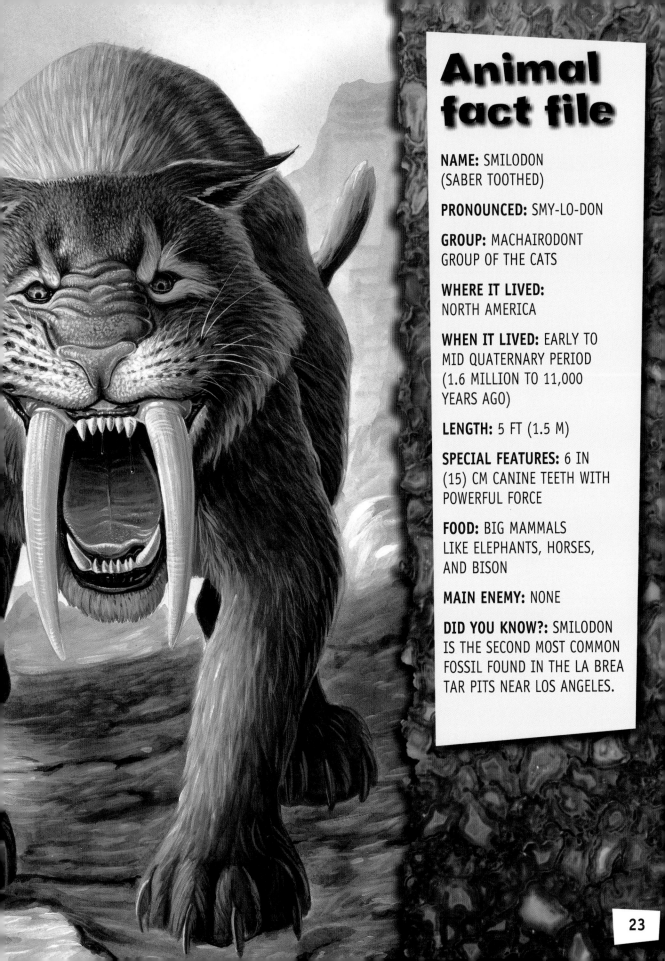

Animal fact file

NAME: SMILODON
(SABER TOOTHED)

PRONOUNCED: SMY-LO-DON

GROUP: MACHAIRODONT
GROUP OF THE CATS

WHERE IT LIVED:
NORTH AMERICA

WHEN IT LIVED: EARLY TO
MID QUATERNARY PERIOD
(1.6 MILLION TO 11,000
YEARS AGO)

LENGTH: 5 FT (1.5 M)

SPECIAL FEATURES: 6 IN
(15) CM CANINE TEETH WITH
POWERFUL FORCE

FOOD: BIG MAMMALS
LIKE ELEPHANTS, HORSES,
AND BISON

MAIN ENEMY: NONE

DID YOU KNOW?: SMILODON
IS THE SECOND MOST COMMON
FOSSIL FOUND IN THE LA BREA
TAR PITS NEAR LOS ANGELES.

Gigantopithecus

The fierce *Gigantopithecus* could rear up to a great height and bellow loudly. It was the biggest ape that ever lived. *Gigantopithecus* made its home in the forested foothills of the mountains of China.

Some people believe *Gigantopithecus* is the Yeti, or abominable snowman, said to live in the Himalayan Mountains.

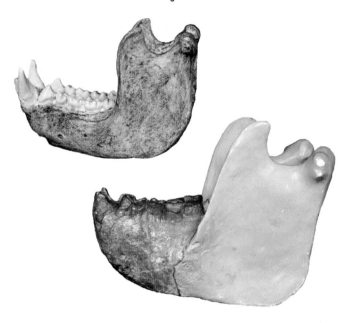

The jawbone at the bottom is a model of *Gigantopithecus's* jawbone. The one at the top is from a gorilla. Gigantopithecus's is much bigger. All that scientists really know about *Gigantopithecus* is the size of its teeth. From the teeth, they can put together the appearance of the whole animal.

Animal fact file

NAME: GIGANTOPITHECUS (GIANT APE)

PRONOUNCED: JI-GAN-TOE-PITH-A-KUSS

GROUP: APES

WHERE IT LIVED: CHINA

WHEN IT LIVED: LATE TERTIARY PERIOD TO EARLY QUATERNARY PERIOD (13 MILLION TO 500,000 YEARS AGO)

HEIGHT: 10 FT (3 M)

SPECIAL FEATURES: LARGE TEETH THAT COULD CHEW TOUGH VEGETATION

FOOD: BAMBOO AND OTHER PLANTS

MAIN ENEMY: NOT KNOWN

DID YOU KNOW?: GIGANTOPITHECUS WAS DISCOVERED IN 1935. A GERMAN PALEONTOLOGIST FOUND FOSSIL TEETH FOR SALE IN A CHINESE MEDICINE SHOP. HE REALIZED THE TEETH CAME FROM AN UNKNOWN PRIMATE.

Australopithecus

Over millions of years, primitive monkeylike animals developed into the monkeys, apes, and humans alive today. *Australopithecus* was an important member of this evolutionary line, and was one of the first apes to walk on two legs. Humans evolved from upright apes like these.

The brain of *Australopithecus* was one-third the size of a human brain. Its teeth and ears are more like those of an ape than a human.

Australopithecus lived on the open plains. It stood upright to see over tall grass. It did not walk on its hands like an ape or use them for climbing like a monkey. It was able to grasp object, although its use of tools was primitive.

Animal fact file

NAME: AUSTRALOPITHECUS (SOUTHERN APE)

PRONOUNCED: OSS-TRAH-LOH--PITH-EK-US

GROUP: HOMINIDS

WHERE IT LIVED: EAST AND SOUTH AFRICA

WHEN IT LIVED: LATE TERTIARY PERIOD TO EARLY QUATERNARY PERIOD (4.4 TO 1.4 MILLION YEARS AGO)

HEIGHT: 4 FT (1.2 M)

SPECIAL FEATURES: THE EARLIEST APE TO WALK ON TWO FEET LIKE A HUMAN

FOOD: PLANTS AND ANIMALS

MAIN ENEMY: BIG CATS LIKE LIONS AND CHEETAHS

DID YOU KNOW?: THERE WERE SEVERAL SPECIES OF AUSTRALOPITHECUS. ALL WERE SMALLER THAN MODERN HUMANS.

Homo

Homo is the genus to which we belong. *Homo erectus* was a species of early human that evolved in Africa about 1.8 million years ago and spread throughout the world. *Homo neanderthalensis* is our closest extinct human relative. Our species—*Homo sapiens*—is the only surviving species.

Homo erectus was one of our ancestors. *Homo* erectus used fire and had tools made of stone, wood, and bone.

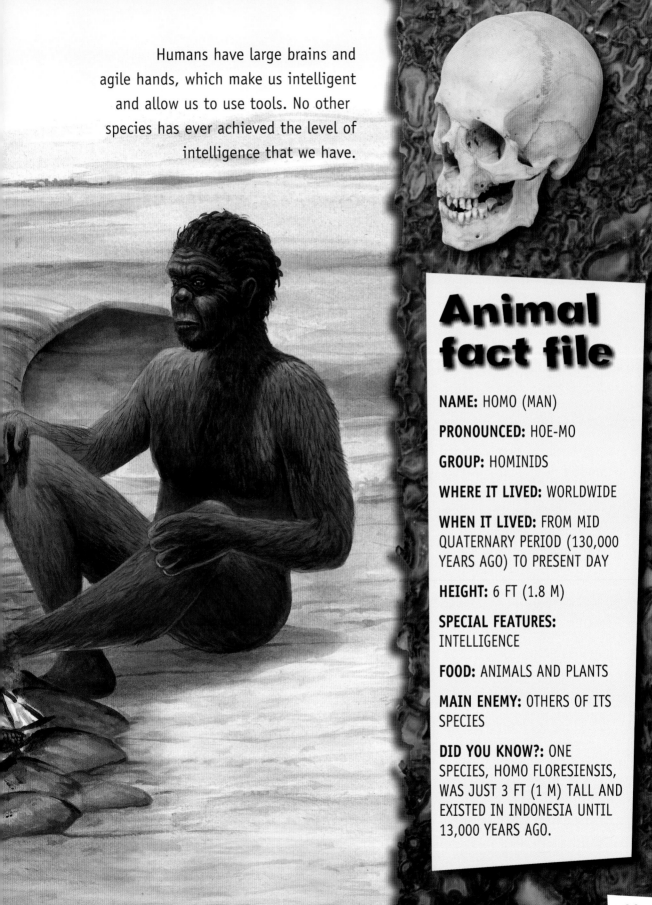

Humans have large brains and agile hands, which make us intelligent and allow us to use tools. No other species has ever achieved the level of intelligence that we have.

Animal fact file

NAME: HOMO (MAN)

PRONOUNCED: HOE-MO

GROUP: HOMINIDS

WHERE IT LIVED: WORLDWIDE

WHEN IT LIVED: FROM MID QUATERNARY PERIOD (130,000 YEARS AGO) TO PRESENT DAY

HEIGHT: 6 FT (1.8 M)

SPECIAL FEATURES: INTELLIGENCE

FOOD: ANIMALS AND PLANTS

MAIN ENEMY: OTHERS OF ITS SPECIES

DID YOU KNOW?: ONE SPECIES, HOMO FLORESIENSIS, WAS JUST 3 FT (1 M) TALL AND EXISTED IN INDONESIA UNTIL 13,000 YEARS AGO.

Animal Families Glossary

Artiodactyls—the group of even-toed hoofed mammals including deer, sheep, pigs, and camels. They have two toes on each foot, giving the "cloven hoof" appearance. They evolved later than the perissodactyls—the odd-toed hoofed mammals.

Glyptodonts—the group of extinct xenarthran mammals that resembled gigantic armadillos. They lived in South America in the Quaternary Period, with one species known from North America.

Hominids—the group of primates that includes human beings and their immediate ancestors, as well as the chimpanzees, gorillas, and orangutans.

Machairodonts—the group of saber-toothed cats. The canine teeth were very long and used as killing weapons. They killed by slashing their prey, not biting it.

Marsupials—a major group of mammals that carry their young in pouches. Today, they are found only in Australia, with the exception of the opossum, which is in North and South America. In the Tertiary Period many of the hunting animals of South America as well as Australia were marsupials.

Perissodactyls—the group of odd-toed hoofed mammals. Modern forms include the horse, the rhinoceros and the tapir. They normally have either one toe or three on each foot. The other hoofed mammal group are the artiodactyls—the even-toed hoofed mammals.

Primates—the group of mammals that includes lemurs, monkeys, apes, and ourselves. Primates have hands and forward-facing eyes.

Ratites—the group of flightless birds. Modern types include the emu and cassowary of Australia, the ostrich of Africa, and the rhea of South America.

Varanids—the group of lizards that include the modern monitor lizards, such as the komodo dragon. Prehistoric forms include the swimming mosasaurs from the Cretaceous Period and the lion-sized lizards that lived in Australia during the Quaternary Period.

Xenarthrans—the group of mammals that includes the anteaters, armadillos, and sloths. They have always been confined to North and South America.

Glossary

Abominable Snowman—an imaginary hairy ape, said to live in the Himalayan Mountains.

Adapted—changing to survive in a particular habitat or weather conditions.

Ambushing—lying in wait out of sight and then making a surprise attack.

Ancestor—an early form of the animal group that lived in the past.

Chain mail—a type of armor made of small rings of metal linked together. It was very flexible.

Compacted hair—a batch of hair that is squashed together so tightly it becomes hard.

Evolution—changes or developments that happen to all forms of life over millions of years, as a result of changes in the environment.

Evolutionary line—the different stages in the development of a certain type of animal.

Flexible—can move in all directions easily.

Fossil—the remains of a prehistoric plant or animal that has been buried for a long time and become hardened in rock.

Ice Age—a period of time when the Earth was covered in ice.

Lichen—a type of plant like moss.

Minerals—found in food and help to keep the body working well.

Mobile—hands and fingers that can grasp food easily.

Neanderthal man—an early type of human who lived millions of years ago.

Peat bog—a type of ground that is damp and covered in moss.

Pouch—the pocket on the front of a marsupial's body.

Prehistory—a time before humans evolved.

Primitive—a very early stage in the development of a species.

Scavenger—an animal that feeds off food other animals have hunted.

Sloth—a very slow moving animal that lives in rainforests.

Tar pit—an area where thick, black, sticky liquid just under the ground bubbles up to the top.

Tropical—a place that is close to the equator and that has a hot, wet climate.

Unique—only one in the world of that type.

Index

A
apes 25, 26, 27
armadillo 14
artiodactyls 17
Australopithecus 26, 27

C
Cambrian Period 5
Carboniferous Period 5
Cenozoic era 5
Coelodonta 20, 21
Cretaceous Period 5

D
Devonian Period 5
Dinornis 8, 9
Doedicurus 14, 15

E
elephants 18, 19

G
Gigantopithecus 24, 25
glyptodonts 14, 15

H
hominids 27, 29
Homo 28, 29
humans 4, 9, 17, 19, 26-29

I
Ice Age 4, 5, 16-18, 20

J
Jurassic Period 5

L
lizards 6, 7

M
machairodonts 23
mammoths 18, 19
Mammuthus 18, 19
marsupials 7, 10, 11
Megalania 6, 7
Megaloceros 16, 17
Megatherium 12, 13
Mesozoic era 5
moa 8, 9

N
Neanderthal man 28

O
Ordovician Period 5

P
Paleozoic era 5
periods 4
perissodactyls 21
Permian Period 5

Q
Quaternary Period 4, 5, 7, 9,
    10, 11, 13, 14, 15, 17, 19,
    21-23, 25, 27, 29

R
ratites 9
reptiles 5, 6

S
saber-tooth cats 22
Silurian Period 5
sloths 12
Smilodon 13, 22, 23

T
Tertiary Period 5, 11, 19,
    25, 27
Thylacoleo 7, 10, 11
Triassic Period 5

V
varanids 7

W
woolly rhinoceros 20, 21

X
xenarthrans 13, 15

Y
Yeti 25

Picture credits

Main image: 6-7, 10-11, 16-17, 18-19, 20-21, 24-25 Simon Mendez; 12-13 Luis Rey; 8-9, 14-15, 22-23, 26-27, 28-29 Chris Tomlin 4TL, 4TR, 5 (Cenozoic Era), 7, 11, 12, 15, 16, 19, 22, 26 Ticktock Media archive; 5 (Mesozoic Era top, Paleozoic Era top) Simon Mendez; 5 (Mesozoic Era center, Paleozoic Era bottom) Luis Rey; 5 (Mesozoic Era bottom) Lisa Alderson; 8, 28 Shutterstock; 24 The Natural History Museum, London; 21© Alexander Shuldiner / Alamy

Every effort has been made to trace the copyright holders and we apologize in advance for any unintentional omissions. We would be pleased to insert the appropriate acknowledgment in any subsequent edition of this publication.